THERE IS NO BUSINESS BUSINESS

A Practical Guide to Knowing
When to Take on a Business Partner
(And When Not To)

PATRICK BURKE

WELLSPRING
North Palm Beach, Florida

wellspring

Cover by Snap Advertising
Interior by Madeline Harris

ISBN: 978-1-63582-099-7 (hardcover)

10   9   8   7   6   5   4   3   2   1

Printed in the United States of America

CONTENTS

PREFACE

"Do I need a partner?" I have been a business adviser for more than thirty-five years, and this is one of the most common questions I am asked by entrepreneurs. This is true whether they are starting their first business or expanding an existing one. This book will not only answer that question, but also tell you how to grow your company while (ideally) maintaining 100 percent ownership or at least a controlling interest. Holding on to as much of your company's ownership as possible and sharing it only when it's absolutely necessary is simple logic. However, in my experience this simple logic gets complicated when business owners allow emotion to dictate whether to go solo or take on a partner.

It seems just when entrepreneurs would benefit most from a clear-eyed assessment of what's needed to succeed, they succumb to the emotional need to partner. I hope the many alternatives to partnering, along with the cautionary stories presented, will convince you to focus instead on how best to operate, grow, and exit *your* company on *your* terms, to maximize *your* return.

ONE: Solo Is OK

I know, literally, there is an "us" in business. However, owning and running a business is one of the few instances in which it is all about you. Your business must compensate you for your time, effort, talent, and capital without the dilution caused by an unnecessary partner.

The census bureau estimates there are 27 million businesses in the United States. Of these, 20 million have only one employee, the owner. There are no figures for companies owned by only one person that have more than one employee, but let's just say it's conservatively another 3 percent. That would mean that roughly 80 percent of businesses in the United States are non-partnerships. (By the way, I will use the term *partnership* to mean any business with more than one owner; I will specify if I am addressing the particular characteristics of a partnership or an LLC as compared to a corporation.) A substantial majority of businesses are owned by one person only. That doesn't make them "right," but it's significant.

The principal goal of a business is to make money. Much good naturally flows from a profitable business, primarily meaningful work for employees. Moreover, a profitable business, which is also a model corporate citizen, invigorates the community by patronizing other local businesses as well as providing charitable contributions and sponsorships. That said, the rest of this book will stress the more mercenary aspects of business.

To establish my bona fides: I've advised more than two hundred start-up businesses, some one owner, some multi-owner; I am not currently a single owner in any business but was a sole proprietor in two of my businesses before I took on partners; I've split from a partner in my principal business of a CPA firm; I've successfully added a partner to that firm; I am currently a partner in six operating businesses and two real estate deals. So I know a thing or two about when two is too many and one is not enough.

Obviously, based on my own track record, there's nothing intrinsically wrong with partnerships. In fact, according to the US Small Business Administration, businesses with multiple owners are likely to survive longer than sole proprietorships. However, I challenge the knee-jerk reaction of starting a business with someone who will also own part of that business without a very compelling reason.

TWO: Two's Company

Of all the reasons to partner with someone in a business, friendship is perhaps the worst. As they say, "If you want a friend, get a dog." I would add, "If you're looking for a partner, join a dance class." In my considerable experience, friendships rarely survive partnerships. You should heed John D. Rockefeller's words: "A friendship founded on a business is a good deal better than a business founded on a friendship." So, if friendship is not an appropriate criterion, when must you partner? That's easy.

You must partner only when your business requires a person with a certain skill you don't possess, and that skill cannot be acquired with money alone. This is the gold standard, so write it in bold letters on your business plan. If you can buy the skill, buy it. As an entrepreneur, you should believe the equity in your business will become your most valuable asset. Therefore, swapping a buyable skill for your equity is potentially a very poor trade. Moreover, knowing how much equity to swap for a skill is very difficult because you must determine the value of a newly formed business as well as the value of the skill. If you are attempting to make the swap before your business is up and running, it may be next to impossible to value the business. Determining your potential partner's relative contribution to your company's ultimate success will be equally difficult. Often the skill a potential partner brings to the partnership is satisfying a short-term rather than a long-term need, and satisfying that need is rarely worth part of your equity. When you consider parting with equity, keep in mind an epic bad deal like the Native Americans swapping Manhattan for twenty-four dollars in beads, because you too could be on the wrong side of the trade.

Assuming your potential partner easily clears the towering "skill only for equity" hurdle, you must also address the inherent unfairness of God-given talents. And, unfortunately, those talents often determine the value a person brings to an enterprise. Most potential partners plan on splitting profits fifty-fifty, despite the long odds that their contributions to the business will be equal.

Think of the salaries of the members of a professional sports team. Salaries are never divided equally among all members of the team. The most talented and valuable players often earn many times the salaries of other players. This is because their contribution to the team's success is often many times that of the other players.

Most businesses are the brainchild of one entrepreneur who believes he or she has found a better answer to some business riddle. Less often, two or more folks come up with such an answer. If the idea is solely yours, and you alone can make it happen, then go it alone. However, when two or more folks are responsible for the idea, then you have found a worthwhile partner. Assuming that the financial commitment of each partner is not the most significant factor in the enterprise's success—and it rarely is—the relative value of the partner's efforts must be determined. This sort of before-the-fact determination of relative value will be difficult, but it's clearly better to get it on the table before money is also on the table. Money always creates its own cloud cover.

Perhaps the best proxy for the relative value of a person's skills to a new business is its relative value to an existing business. An example of this analysis would be determining all partners' salaries and the equity percentage they will own by reviewing the relative salaries the partners would demand if they were hired by an existing business to provide the same services they plan on providing to the new business. Implicit in this analysis is the relative difficulty of finding someone with each potential partner's skill set.

Now is probably a good time to address the threshold question: Are you the business partner type? Some people are born to go solo, particularly if that's what you've done for most of your business career. So examine your conscience to determine if you will be able to share decision making and tolerate the practically inevitable disparity between your effort and efficacy and your partner's, and how this disparity may not be reflected in your profit sharing percentages. If you know yourself and this scenario would be intolerable, it may be best to grossly overpay for a needed skill or find another business you can do alone. This caveat should not be taken lightly. Many of my most successful clients are still 100 percent owned by the founder even after more than thirty years in business.

Lest you think this desire to go it alone will wane significantly over time, recently I presided over a transaction in which a seventy-two-year-old entrepreneur and founder of a successful manufacturing business purchased his former business from his daughter and her husband. He believed they were not operating it properly, notwithstanding near-record profitability. He told me he just couldn't bear seeing the business operate at less than optimal efficiency. Knowing him, and watching him in action for more than thirty years, I am confident that he will improve performance. I also know he will be more comfortable operating the business and giving money to his daughter and her husband than allowing them to earn money in "his" business.

There is a non-partnership solution that may be best for both you and a valuable employee. Often an employee will insist on becoming an owner as a condition of either initial or continued employment. This is sometimes, but not often, a valid request (recall the "skill only for equity" hurdle). However, more often, it's an issue that can be resolved without making this person an actual owner in your business. Many times an employee's request for equity is really a desire for a long-term wealth-building opportunity outside of the company's retirement plan and her own savings. If an employee's efforts are helping the company become more profitable and more valuable, perhaps you should consider allowing her to share in this incremental value.

Through a vehicle known as a stock appreciation right (SAR), you can provide an employee with a wealth-building opportunity without giving up actual equity in your business. With the help of your lawyer and accountant, your company can adopt a SAR plan for one or more of your employees that will allow participation in the increase in value of your company over some set period of time. For example, if you currently value your company using an appropriate industry metric at $2 million, you can draft an SAR plan that allows key employees to participate in 10 percent of the increase in value over $2 million at the rate of 1 percent per year for the next 10 years. In this example, if the company doubles in value from $2 million to $4 million, the participants will earn $200,000 (10 percent of the $2 million increase) over the 10-year period. The amount earned can either be paid immediately to the participants at the end of the 10-year period or paid over, say, 3 years to help protect company cash flow.

Try as you might to go it alone, bringing on a partner may be your very best opportunity for success, and that's OK. Just make sure every other avenue is fully explored first.

THREE: Choosing Wisely

If you've determined you must partner, you must also address whether you and your prospective partner are a good fit. Since this relationship is much like a marriage, in my experience there's at least a fifty-fifty chance it will unravel. The mutual evaluation process of potential partners should be undertaken with great care. Ideally, there should be a proper courting period, during which some extremely important questions must be asked and answered.

Drive is the one trait that is universal among successful entrepreneurs. You have it even if you don't realize it. Does your prospective partner match your level of passion for the business? And, is he or she committed to continually improving the skills that made him or her indispensable? If the answer to these questions is *no*, you're doomed. I would suggest you and your potential partner take a personality test such as the DiSC to see if you're compatible. You don't need to be equally driven; that's likely a separate problem. Entrepreneurs are passionate and are much more successful when they partner with others who share their passion.

Next—and this will be difficult—consider whether your prospective partner is too rich or too poor to go into business with you. If your partner is too rich, success won't mean as much to him as it does to you, so it will be hard to match up your levels of passion. Further, fear is perhaps the best motivator, and if your partner is independently wealthy, success, while a goal, may not be necessary for his well-being. Your fight-or-flight instincts won't match. On the other hand, a partner who is too poor will likely be unable to match your cash in the event of a capital call. Needing additional cash is a highly likely occurrence, particularly with a start-up. Moreover, if you end up borrowing from a bank, you and your partner will likely be required to sign personally, and under the terms of the note, you'll be joint and severally liable. This means the bank may look to one or both of you to satisfy the debt.

If your partner is significantly less well-off than you and the company can't pay off its note, the bank will go after your assets first and let you pursue your partner's assets. So, as uncomfortable as this may be, swap personal financial statements to make sure you're financially compatible.

Even though under state, corporate, and limited liabilities statues you are not responsible for your partner's actions beyond your investment in your business, you should consider whether your prospective partner is someone of the highest moral character. If you're judged by the company you keep, you are judged even more critically by who you choose as your partner. Making this determination will involve tough discussions. And even though it may seem intrusive, I would suggest mutual credit and background checks. Nothing promotes full disclosure like complete transparency. Even though this may not literally be the case with your business, you should be proud to have your partner's name next to yours on a sign swinging from the front of your establishment.

On the risk continuum from riverboat gambler to actuary, where does your potential partner fall? There is no better time to discuss long-term goals than before you start. You might see your joint business as a potential juggernaut that can be expanded significantly. Your partner, however, may see it as a lifestyle business that provides little more than a good and high-paying job. Such a divergence in goals is often based on relative risk profiles. Some partners seek to circumscribe risk, and may see little reason to take a chance when things are good. On the other hand, some partners see good times as a good time to double down.

A client of mine I'll call Tom, an engineer, developed a proprietary machining technique that allowed power plants to cut maintenance downtime drastically. The technique required a skilled machinist and since Tom wasn't a machinist, he hired John, a machinist, and made him a 50 percent partner in his business. The business started off in Salt Lake City and planned to expand to Cincinnati to be closer to Midwest and East Coast customers. Of course, this expansion meant doubling not only operating costs but also the entire manufacturing process. At this point, John got scared and refused to sign personally on a larger line of credit. Due to this impasse, he invoked the "cutthroat" buy-sell provision in their partnership agreement. Under the terms of this provision, partner A names a price and partner B decides if, at that price, he is a buyer or seller. John elected to have Tom name the price. (Such a provision is supposed to enforce fairness, since if the price is too high, the other party will sell, and if it's too low the other party will buy.) I attended the meeting with Tom, who was understandably nervous. He had worked very hard with me and his bank to determine a fair price that would be high enough that he was fairly certain his partner would sell. It worked. We settled on $1 million, John took his cash and Tom moved forward, eventually doubling the size of the business and selling it for $4 million. Later, he bought it back for $3 million, built it even larger, and sold it for $6 million to his management team. Although Tom made enough money on those "trades" to never work again, he went on to start five more businesses. He is still operating four of them (one failed—you guessed it, bad partner). So, make sure you share the same BHAGs—big hairy audacious goals—as Jim Collins outlines in his book *Build to Last*, or, like Tom, you could end up in your lawyer's office with your business's life on the line.

Finally, does your partner clearly understand what each of you will be responsible for accomplishing within your business? A successful business, distilled to its essence, is team members executing processes. The value of these processes is judged by the other members of the team on their relative contribution to the success of the enterprise and, ultimately, by customers who decide whether or not to buy. Therefore, even with partners, or maybe even especially with partners, it's critical to define your roles as specifically as possible, and hold each other accountable. This sounds easy, and at the beginning, it is. One partner, we'll call her the founder, is likely a great salesperson. She is a natural. Customers love her, referral sources keep her phone ringing, and she makes it all look too easy. True rainmakers are like that.

Inevitably, the other partner, we'll call him the operator, thinks sales is little more than glorified entertainment and believes operations are the key to the current and continued success of the business. He believes that because of the founder's orientation, the company puts a higher value on sales than operations. Therefore, he too begins selling. The outcome: poor closing rates on his sales calls and backsliding operating results—clearly a disaster! Linebackers don't throw passes just because they want to be more valuable to the team. They follow the game plan, make tackles, and knock down passes, and the team wins—the only stat that counts. Like many others, this partner issue can be mostly avoided with a good partnership agreement or employment contract (much more on this later).

FOUR: "But you don't understand, I need the money."

Most entrepreneurs underestimate not only how much money their new venture will need but also the amount of money they can raise without investors or partners. When I am asked to review a business plan, I often remark, "Funny how no business ever loses money next year." Most entrepreneurs will give themselves the first year to work out the kinks. By the second year it's positive cash flow and on to Easy Street, or at least a neighborhood nearby. This is generally unwarranted optimism. The most sophisticated entrepreneurs do what I call "solving for negative cash." By preparing a monthly cash flow model, along with a balance sheet, an entrepreneur can determine not only how much cash is needed and when, but also how much bank financing will be available to the company at any given time based on its equity. Translated: A company can often support more bank financing than one would think. Understanding the gap between negative cash and bank financing is critical because it indicates the money that must somehow be raised elsewhere.

The typical reaction is to fill this gap with a financial partner. However, as you might guess, that's the last place you should go. The cheapest money is your own. Although you are potentially giving up record returns in the stock market, those returns should pale in comparison to the future value of the equity in your own business. If you don't believe this, don't proceed. No matter the source of the financing, the lender or investor will view your confidence level in your business as proportionate to what you have invested in it. Investors and lenders will look unfavorably on your business if you provide only sweat equity or a level of cash investment disproportionately small as compared to your net worth. If the failure of your business doesn't represent a near-existential threat to your lifestyle, investors or lenders will view you as having too little skin in the game, and rightly so.

In addition to the obvious capital source of your personal investment assets, you have other ready sources, including equity in your home and money you can borrow from your retirement account through a mechanism known as a ROBS (rollover for business start-ups). With a ROBS, you may use money from your 401(k) or other retirement accounts to invest in your business rather than in more traditional investments such as mutual funds. Although ROBS is fairly restrictive, it is clearly worth exploring before selling equity to or borrowing money from an outsider under what may be onerous terms.

You also may be able to convince strategic suppliers to provide liberal payment terms, thus decreasing the amount of up-front cash necessary. Or if your business provides a new solution, some customers may be willing to either pay in advance or sign a long-term contract that guarantees you significant cash flow in the future. As an added bonus, early adopters usually provide invaluable insight into how to improve your product or service. In general, customers love getting in on the ground floor. Counterintuitively, often the easiest sales are to these initial customers, who many times become some of your best and most loyal customers. I have retained almost all the clients I first sold in 1984 when my value proposition as a green, twenty-eight-year-old CPA/attorney was based more on my (mostly irrational) exuberance than on skill or a track record.

Bootstrapping (paying suppliers as you go) is the most effective way to stretch your capital. The more you can bootstrap at the beginning, as you achieve market validation, increase your market value, and build equity on your own, the less dilution you will suffer if you must raise outside money later. So keeping costs low by leasing equipment, office sharing, and simply using the assets you have reduces the cash you will need up front. All new business owners see themselves in the corner office, with their car parked next to the flagpole in front of a beautiful building, but unless you are starting a business in which image is the most critical success factor, eschew image in favor of cash savings.

"OK," you say, "I still have a sizable financial gap." If that's truly the case, and it often is, there are other funding sources available, which I will outline from most to least desirable.

Before we proceed, you'll need to understand a few things about the Securities Act of 1933. This act was passed in the wake of the stock market crash of 1929, when many investors lost money to sponsors who promoted investment returns that were never realized. The Act defines a security and requires sellers of securities to disclose all the risks to potential investors so that they can make an informed decision on whether or not to invest. A security includes any arrangement involving the investment of money in an enterprise in which profits come solely through the efforts of others. Under the Act, any sale of a security must be registered at the federal and usually the state levels, unless the sponsor or the transaction qualifies for an exemption from registration. However, registration can be avoided if all investors participate unanimously in decisions involving the investment. This unanimous participation requirement is generally so unattractive to entrepreneurs that it is rarely utilized. Compliance with these rules is necessary for raising money from any outside investors, except private equity or venture capital firms, who are capable of doing their own due diligence (more on that later).

The most typical non-founder source of funds is commonly and pejoratively known as "family, friends, and fools," or FFF. According to the crowdsourcing website Fundable, friends and family are the major funding source for all entrepreneurs, investing more than $60 billion in new ventures each year. The average amount is only $23,000, but every little bit helps. Investments from FFF are best structured as a loan, as you don't want family and friends as partners any more than you want other business partners (maybe even less)! Interestingly, some professional investors see the lack of funds from family and friends in a business as an indication of the founder's lack of confidence in his or her business. After all, why should an outsider invest in you if your family won't?

The exemption from registration associated with acquiring funds from your family and friends is Rule 506(b) of Regulation D of the Securities Act, which allows solicitation of known investors. This exemption disallows both general and internet solicitation. However, it does allow up to thirty-five non-accredited investors and unlimited accredited investors. The SEC defines an accredited investor as a person who has $1 million in assets, excluding the primary residence, or $200,000 in yearly income for a single person, or $300,000 in yearly income for a married couple. Also, under the FFF exemption there is no limitation on the offering size.

It's best when dealing with FFF to ask for a specific amount to achieve a specific rolled-up milestone, after which the payment to the investor will commence. This ensures a closed-end deal, which is always preferred by both parties. It's critical to remember that no investment is a gift; thus, the inherent risk of a start-up (more than 70 percent fail in the first five years) must be clearly communicated. Often, this type of investment yields unexpected return in the form of unsolicited but sound advice. Remember, people with extra money to invest are generally sophisticated and have connections and experiences that may be helpful to you and your enterprise. This reminds me of one of my favorite business truisms, passed on to me by one of my mentors, Ted, a ninety-two-year-old, still active entrepreneur. Ted told me that the first time he tried to raise money from his dad, he received advice. After a few successes, he once again approached his dad, only this time it was for advice, and instead he came away with money. I suppose the moral of the story is if you're shooting for success, accept all investments—sage advice included, because it may eventually lead to cash.

Before we move on to professional investors, we'll address another, newer source of cash: crowdfunding. This is a form of online financing. The 2012 Jumpstart Our Business Startups Act (JOBS Act) legalized solicitation of retail investors through crowdfunding. As with Rule 506(b), crowdfunding has its own rules and regulations, which must be followed carefully. The biggest difference from Rule 506(b) is that crowdfunding allows marketing to outsiders through the use of a funding portal. The solicitation, also known as an offering, is limited to $1 million.

To utilize this exemption from registration, the issuer must adhere to the terms of the agreement on the crowdfunding site (examples include: Kickstarter, Indiegogo, and GoFundMe). In addition, issuers must follow the copyright, trademark, and patent laws when providing information to potential investors. In summary, crowdfunding is a way to fund that's technical, but allows you to solicit broadly, as long as you don't need more than $1 million.

The last avenue for soliciting outside funds without registration and without professional investors is offerings under Rule 506(c), which went into effect in 2013. Offerings under this rule are similar to crowdfunding; however, marketing and disclosure are not done through a funding portal, but rather via social media and television. Unlike with offerings under Rule 506(b) and crowdfunding, only accredited investors may buy, and just as with the family and friends offerings, there is no dollar limit on the offering size.

It is extremely important to note that your liability under the Rule 506(b) and (c) offerings is covered under the strong anti-fraud Rule 10b-5 of the Securities Act under which you can be subject to both civil and criminal liability. While liability under crowdfunding is covered by both Rule 10b-5 and Section 12(a)(2) of the Securities Act—which allows investors to sue for their entire net investment. The issuer, its officers and directors, and anyone selling the offering can be held responsible under this section. If all this sounds a bit scary, it can be. As my fourth-grade teacher, Sister Michelle, was fond of saying, "A word to the wise is sufficient."

These federal and state securities laws change frequently, so check with your advisers or call me before utilizing any of these fund-raising techniques.

Once you've exhausted all the possibilities of raising money from nonprofessional sources, it's time to move on to the pros. These are the folks who not only provide money in exchange for equity, they also provide advice that should supercharge growth and, more important, value. These investors exchange their capital for equity they plan to turn back into cash over a relatively short time horizon, generally five to seven years. Such investors come in three basic flavors: angels, private equity, and venture capital.

Angels come in two varieties: organized angel groups and solo angels. Angels are by far the most common source of professional start-up funding, investing in 55,000 such companies each year, versus only 1,500 by venture capital investors. In 2014, angel investments exceeded venture capital funding by $3 billion. Only about 7 percent of angels are part of an organized angel group, so you'll have to network with your mentors and your professional team to identify the angel funding source that will be interested in your industry and your idea. Most angels are professionals with full-time jobs and are more likely to make decisions through trusted referrals than active due diligence. Further, they are prone to making gut-level decisions, so prepare to sell yourself—hard!

Your choice of angel depends on what you're looking for in an investor. Some angels wish to be activist investors, being heavily involved in day-to-day decisions. However, I find most prefer to act more like a member of the board of directors, following the NIFO model (nose in, fingers out).

Although it's likely these angel investors are more casual, to sell them you must have a good business plan that includes personal references, and projected financial statements that you must know backward and forward. In my experience it's very dangerous to ask for a number when you don't know your own. Which brings us to the most critical and often most contested number: your company's valuation. You will be asking for a specific amount of cash for a specific percentage ownership in your business. As a result, you'll need to arrive at your number and be able to defend it by utilizing valuations of companies in your industry, as well as business valuation metrics that are usually determined by a multiple of cash flow. Inevitably, this is a tough negotiation, so be prepared.

The metrics used for the initial value of your company will likely be the same when the angel exits your business. In general, angels hope to yield a return that is 3 to 4 times their original investment. For example, if the current valuation is $250,000 based on 5 times the current cash flow of $50,000, cash flow would need to increase to $200,000 for the investment to quadruple. If you can't realistically realize growth at that rate or better, in a 5- to 7-year time horizon, you may need to return to the non-pros for your cash, because it will be difficult to attract an angel investor.

Finally, be nice to your angels, because the most likely outcome is they will not see their money again (sorry, but it's true). Ask if you can help them in some way with their business or other investments. You never know when you may want to ask for their help again—and it's just the right thing to do.

I have made two true angel investments, both of which failed. These losses taught me to never again invest in a company in which my education, experience, and expertise added little or no value to the enterprise. One of the investments was a rent-to-own business; the other was an industrial cleaning product distributor. Both were legitimate businesses operated by illegitimate executives, which taught me another expensive lesson: Spend as much time and effort evaluating the operators as you do the operations. If you are trying to attract angel investment capital and are less than squeaky-clean, you must disclose this up front, because it will be found out. If this means you must go back to your non-pros, so be it.

The next link up the investor food chain is private equity and venture capital investors. I'll address them together because they operate under very similar models. Venture capitalists invest in new concepts, while private equity firms invest in growth companies or buyouts. Both types of firms act as general partners in investment partnerships. The limited partners are very high-net-worth individuals and institutions, such as insurance companies and pension funds who invest capital in the funds. A fund usually lasts five to seven years, after which it is liquidated. At that time the general partners receive a return on both their cash invested (they invest alongside the limited partners) and time, whereas the limited partners' return is based strictly on cash invested. Since these are risky investments, limited partners expect an annual return of 20 percent or more.

To achieve returns at this level, the partnerships shoot for investments in companies that could yield four to five times their initial investment (these firms use leverage, borrowing 50 percent or more of their investment, thereby increasing the yield on their equity). Like angel investments, many private equity and venture capital investments fail outright. To make up for these failures, the fund's portfolio companies must have a very high upside potential. So if your company is based on an idea that can't grow at the rate private equity or venture capitalist firms require, you'll need to look elsewhere for your funding.

You should think of private equity and venture capital as transitional capital. Your own patient capital will likely outlast the time horizon of the private equity or venture capital firm. Therefore, you need to understand the firm's fund cycle so you can plan for its inevitable exit. In addition, the following areas should be a part of your due diligence on the firm you're negotiating with: Be sure you and the partner assigned to your company have the necessary chemistry and trust; make sure the firm adds significant value through specific knowledge of your industry; and research the track record of the firm—you want to be associated with a proven winner.

Once you have chosen a firm, you will also need to negotiate the structure of the investment. The firm's investment can take the form of common or preferred stock (which, as the name implies, means a preferred return ahead of your common shares). This negotiation must be done with the aid of seasoned professionals because it will ultimately determine how much of your company's upside you'll keep. Lastly, governance issues such as the number of board seats you will have compared to the investor must be negotiated.

As you would guess, very few companies meet private equity's or venture capital's criteria; in fact, only one in four hundred deals reviewed by these firms receive an investment. In order to meet their demanding criteria, your company must have strong recurring revenue driven by what the investor believes is a strategic advantage. Further, the firm needs to believe that through its superior experience, it can ensure your company's advantage is both sustainable and scalable.

Obviously, to meet the firms' standards you'll need a compelling and well-defined growth story and a detailed plan to implement it, paying particular attention to how the new capital will be used. Finally, the valuation, just like with an angel investor, must be negotiated hard during this process.

Well, that's the quick tour of the professional investor waterfront. The good news is, unlike almost all partners, these investors get in only when they see a way out. The way out will involve either you or someone else buying them out. If it's you, you're on your own again. If it's someone else, such as another investor or a strategic buyer from your industry, the process must be repeated.

FIVE: Caveat Emptor

OK, now let's put the shoe on the other foot and assume you are buying into an existing business. Here, the most important caveat is—and write this in indelible marker on your palm—don't buy part of a business that you wouldn't buy all of. Treating every dollar as though it were your only dollar is the only way to ensure the proper mind-set when investing in an existing business. Amateur investors are generally far too cavalier when buying into an existing business. They tend to take the current owner's claims at face value and wrongly believe their involvement and cash are the only ingredients necessary for the business's success or greater success. This sort of business narcissism is dangerous and expensive.

I hope the previous chapter's explanation of the hoops you must jump through to separate potential investors from their money provide you with the template for your own level of due diligence. The key word should be *circumspect*. If your awkward-meter is unusually sensitive and asking pointed questions pegs it in the red zone, delegate. Have your CPAs lead a due diligence team. They've done this before and enjoy snooping (which, after all, is their job). Professional skeptics can obtain information, interpret it, and divine business truths you would miss on your own.

If you, or perhaps a friend, have ever tried to buy a business, you know it is extremely time consuming, frustrating, and usually unsuccessful. Finding just the right business (see my book *Exit Velocity* for a further discussion of this) is much more than simply finding one for sale at the right price. The most important variable is whether you can add something to the business that will make it more profitable and sustainable. To determine if you can add value to a business, you need to carefully assess how you fit into the business. This may seem obvious, but based on how often I've seen investors buy into absolutely the wrong business, it is not. Evaluate your skills, interests, education, and most important, your experience, and only consider buying into a business that meshes with what you do well. Further, make sure the company's already established image and culture are topflight. Since these intangibles were built over time, they will be next to impossible to change. Lastly, only consider companies that are on a positive trajectory. Failing companies are projects for turnaround professionals, and such projects should not be "tried at home."

Having narrowed the scope of your search, it may be helpful to then broaden it by including businesses that are seeking investment partners rather than 100 percent buyers. If you are planning on being an active rather than a silent partner in your target business, your ability to add value and your fit is just as important as it would be if you were buying 100 percent.

Perhaps the worst buying decision I witnessed was made years ago by a friend, Vince, a banker by trade, who insisted on buying into a failing neighborhood restaurant. Vince believed he could transform this greasy spoon into a thriving establishment by turning it into a pizza parlor. Now, this was before the explosion of national pizza chains, so it didn't seem patently ill-advised. But it was. Pizza didn't sell any better in this down-market location than the blue plate specials did. After I helped Vince shut down this failed retail experiment, I asked why he, a Cincinnatian of German descent, believed he had some special insight into pizza. His response: "Even though I didn't have a killer recipe, my family and I ate pizza at a different parlor nearly every Sunday. So I thought I knew what it took to be a pizza magnate." Unfortunately, not quite "easy as pie."

Another way to buy into an existing business is to find a business owner who is seeking a partner to facilitate his or her exit from the business. I have put together a number of transactions in which the new partner's buy-in serves as the old partner's buyout. If this is really what you're seeking, don't assume the seller shares your vision. Instead start with the end in mind and establish upfront both a timetable for the buyout as well as a valuation metric for the buyout price. I have set up deals in which after, say, three years of working together, the buyer has the right to buy out the original owner at a set price (a call option); meanwhile, the original owner has a similar right to require the buyer to buy out his or her interest at a set price (a put option). With this arrangement, the partners remain partners after the first three years only if they mutually agree. This sort of plan requires additional work at the beginning and some tough conversations, but setting the correct mutual expectations up front is always far easier than negotiating an agreement post-buy-in.

Unlike buying 100 percent of a business, in which the transaction is usually structured as a sale of assets, buying into an existing business means you'll be buying stock if the enterprise is a corporation, or an interest if the enterprise is an LLC or partnership. As a result, you immediately share in the risks and liabilities of the company, at least up to your initial investment. Therefore, as part of your due diligence, you need to determine if there are judgements, liens, or lawsuits that are not disclosed in the company's financial statements. In addition, you need to understand all the business governance documents, such as the operating and employment agreements. Even though the current owners of the company have negotiated their mutual rights and responsibilities and memorialized them in these agreements, your deal does not have to mirror theirs. You won't be able to change the current owners' deal with respect to each other; however, you can negotiate your own deal because new money is generally tied to new terms.

Whether your money is being utilized to purchase a partner's interest or in exchange for a newly issued interest has a significant bearing on the percentage of the company you receive. I didn't examine this issue as part of the analysis of raising money from professional partners because I thought it would be more impactful if it was about your money. As with a purchase of 100 percent of a business, a buy-in to an existing business will involve negotiating the value of the enterprise. If, for example, the enterprise is valued at $1 million and you're buying 20 percent from an existing partner, the price will be $200,000.

On the other hand, if that same $200,000 is invested directly into the same company in exchange for an interest, the company's new "post-money" value is $1.2 million. So your $200,000 buys only 16.7 percent ownership, because in essence you are buying into some of your own equity.

Sometimes buy-in transactions are initiated by the company. This most often happens when key employees are asked to buy-in, are offered equity as part of the company's compensation program, or a combination of the two. The issues associated with these types of buy-ins are really no different than with an outside buyer except that, because of the employee's familiarity with the company, the due diligence is easier and faster. Although I have mostly avoided tax issues in our analysis, the tax implications of buying into a company at a bargain price or receiving equity in exchange for labor are critical. These transactions are covered under IRS Section 83, which requires the excess of the value received by the service provider over the price paid, if any, to be included in the recipient's gross income. The only exception to this rule is the award of a profits-only interest in a partnership or LLC to an employee. This is because an interest in future profits is considered to have no present monetary value.

So, in some ways, buying into an existing business is less risky because the people who have always run it continue to run it. On the other hand, they may be just the folks who have been holding the company back. One of my favorite and (I believe) most valid business maxims is: "The people who got you in trouble will never get you out of it." So, as this chapter's title suggests, buyer beware.

SIX: The Correct Horse for the Correct Course

As is obvious by now, I have a strong prejudice against operating companies starting out as partnerships. However, I believe there are businesses for which partnerships are the correct entity from the outset, namely investment partnerships. The best example is a real estate partnership, so most of my analysis will focus on issues associated with this type of entity.

The most common obstacle to overcome when investing in real estate is capital. Forming a partnership with other investors allows the partners to combine capital to invest in larger real estate deals, which in turn mitigates risk—an all-important consideration. Think of the reduction in risk associated with owning a twenty-unit apartment building compared to a two-family home. Also, more partners means more cash will be available if a cash injection is needed sometime in the future—this happens most of the time.

As with an operating company, it's wise to choose your real estate partners based on complementary skills. So if you're a skilled repair and maintenance person, choosing a partner who's a leasing guru certainly increases your chances of success by reducing costs and vacancies. As with all partnerships, correct division of labor and accountability is needed to succeed.

Unlike with the acquisition of an operating company, it is much easier to make an informed decision on the value of a real estate investment, because you can compare the target property to comparable properties. However, when making the decision to invest, nothing beats a powerful network of contacts, including banks, real estate lawyers, brokers, and most important, other real estate investors. Although everyone makes a bad deal now and then, pros make fewer. That's how they become pros. So focus on identifying and adding pros to your network and follow their lead and advice.

A partnership or LLC is the most suitable entity for ownership of real estate because of the almost limitless ability to allocate profits and losses. I like to say if you can draw it up on the back of a napkin, you can accomplish it with a partnership or LLC. In addition to the flexibility in the allocation of profit and loss, partnerships and LLCs can provide additional flexibility through the use of guaranteed payments, which allow partners to be paid out of the partnership's operations for their services before profit or loss is allocated to the rest of the partners. For example, if one of the partners provides maintenance and property management services to the partnership, the partnership can pay that partner for his or her services and that payment is deducted in calculating the profit or loss which is then allocated to all of the partners.

In general, ownership percentages are based on relative capital contributions. However, if bank debt is used and only one partner is personally guaranteeing the partnership debt, the partners can agree that the guaranteeing partner's profit and loss percentages can reflect the additional risk of signing personally. For example, if two partners put up $100,000 each toward the purchase of a $1 million building, and only one partner signs personally on the $800,000 mortgage note, he or she could be allocated an extra 20 percent of both the operating and eventual sale profits as compensation for the additional risk of the guarantee. The ability to shift risk and reward this way can be done only within an LLC or partnership. Corporations—especially S corporations, in which the profits and losses pass through directly to the shareholders—have stricter tax rules when it comes to allocating profits and losses. In fact, profit distributions from an S corporation must match stock ownership percentages, or the IRS may revoke the S election, resulting in the corporation becoming a C corporation, which is an inappropriate vehicle for real estate ownership.

Now is probably a good time to discuss investing in publicly marketed real estate limited partnerships. The upside to these investment vehicles is you are investing with true real estate pros, so much of the investment and execution risk is reduced. As you would expect, with the reduced risk comes reduced return. The general partners are compensated for their time, expertise, and capital contributions. The limited partners are compensated based strictly on the capital they contributed. In my experience these deals have become more fair in recent years because the public has become more sophisticated. The old adage—before the deal the general partners have the experience and the limited partners have the money, and after the deal, the limited partners have the experience (usually bad) and the general partners have the money is not as true as it once was. But there are still some shrewd general partners out there, so be wary of these deals. Invest only after you have performed significant due diligence on the general partners.

With real estate investments it's best to begin with the end in mind, because at the time of sale your relative profit sharing percentages are most important. Therefore, if you believe one or more of the partners may play a larger role in achieving a higher sales price for the property, you can address the compensation of this partner's efforts up front by adding performance provisions to the partnership agreement. For example, if the leasing agent partner has done an excellent job keeping rents up and vacancies down, you could allocate him or her a higher percentage of the profit on the sale above a certain hurdle rate return on the partners' invested capital.

I've been involved with four real estate partnerships personally, and have helped set up scores of others. Both of my first two deals (an industrial building and a small apartment complex) made money but were too small for the number of partners involved. As a result, the returns on my investments were small compared to the capital and time I invested. (I did all the accounting and tax work free; I never did this again.) The other two are office buildings, one of which houses my accounting firm. Both buildings have nice cash flow, and thanks to good partnership agreements, I have zero partner issues. Frankly, even though I could have done the two office building deals on my own, it was more prudent to spread the risk.

Unlike with operating companies in which, to quote another old adage, "too many cooks spoil the broth," I believe the opposite is true with investment partnerships. Here the adage "Many hands make light work" is more applicable.

SEVEN: Perfect Match

Although this book is mostly a cautionary tale, I would like to change the tone and tell you the story of a highly successful partnership and why it works. In 1991 a client, we'll call him Carl, came to me and asked me to sell his company, which we'll call RCM. He had AIDS, and at that time, there was little he could do but mark time. Before starting RCM Carl worked for a health-care collection agency. Through his hospital contacts, he learned that hospitals regularly miss charges when treatment information is transferred from the patient's medical record to the hospital's bill. These missed charges can be re-billed to the payer, generally an insurance company. Carl created RCM to find and re-bill these missed charges. RCM charged the hospital a fee based on a percentage of the additional amounts the hospital received as a result of the re-bill. The company had only a handful of employees and Carl was running it part-time from the sunroom off the kitchen in his home.

I mentioned the company to my older brother, Mike, a lawyer, who had recently told me about a new client of his, Jim, who was in the nursing home industry. Because of Jim's medical billing experience via the nursing home business, I thought he might be interested in buying RCM, and I told Mike to run it by Jim. Sure enough, Jim was interested, and he hired Mike's law firm and my CPA firm to perform due diligence and determine a fair price. Jim and Carl both liked our number, so a deal was struck. At this point, Jim approached Mike and me and asked us if we'd like to partner with him on the deal. Jim thought with his medical background, Mike's legal background, and my accounting background, we'd be able to grow this company and maybe even make a few bucks. He followed the gold standard described in chapter two for whether to take on a partner and decided to partner with people with certain skills he did not possess and could not acquire with money alone. Just as important, becoming partners was an easy decision because we knew and respected each other's skills as well as our mutual ethical approach to business.

Our partnership had a rough start because we lost our largest client during our first month of operation. This loss turned into a blessing because it allowed us to renegotiate the purchase price with Carl (we still owed 50 percent of the agreed price) and it highlighted our need for a topflight sales executive. Enter John, a seasoned and successful salesperson who cut his teeth with Ross Perot's EDS, selling data-processing systems. John went all in, borrowing money and buying in as a partner. From the outset, each partner performed the functions connected to his profession on a consulting basis, except John, who became the company's first full-time salesperson.

Initially the results were anything but spectacular, but with Jim, Mike, and me acting as board members first and consultants as needed, we were able focus on the big picture while minimizing professional fees. As we grew, we decided it was time to hire talented and experienced executives to handle the day-to-day operations and assist the board in long-term planning. To that end, we hired Ty as CEO and Frank as COO and turned them loose with only occasional NIFO (nose in fingers out) guidance. As a result, the company has flourished. The handful of "sunroom" employees has grown to a national workforce of more than five hundred people operating in all fifty states. Over the years, the company has added several new lines of business to help hospitals with their revenue cycle management. And the partnership is still together and going strong.

Why did this particular partnership work? Mainly, I believe, it is due to the partners' alignment of interest. With the exception of John, none of us were looking to the business for our livelihood. Rather, we all saw it as a long-term investment vehicle, and as a result, we were very patient. We didn't panic when we lost a few key clients over the years. And we didn't get stars in our eyes and sell out early when the healthcare market got frothy after 2010. Each partner did what he did best. God smiled on us a bit, and we now have a fast-growing, well-run business. Each year the company is not only more profitable, but more valuable.

Like most success stories, I probably made this sound easier than it really was. But just know that combining capital with partners making the highest and best use of their skills, and deploying both in the correct vertical, equals big-time success!

EIGHT: Good Fences Make Good Neighbors

Just as good fences make good neighbors, good operating agreements make good partners. Although it's impossible to prevent all disputes, good agreements should, as my law school legal drafting professor liked to say, "visualize" all likely events. Drafting the appropriate agreement can make the difference between smooth sailing and ruined friendships and tarnished reputations. All litigation associated with a business divorce is contentious, lengthy, and expensive. However, it is mostly avoidable if, right from the start, you and your partners have tough conversations about how you want to handle potential conflicts.

A handshake and a "We'll always be fair to each other" may seem fine when you start out, but the handshake may turn into fisticuffs if your relationship with your partner goes south. In my experience partnerships work best when the business is performing at a "so-so" level. If the business is hitting on all eight cylinders, there are probably more profits to split than the partners expected. Inevitably one of the partners believes, usually correctly, that her contribution to the success of the enterprise is greater than her ownership. If this is true, the converse is also true, and one or more of the other partners is being over-rewarded. The ensuing friction is usually incendiary. There is also likely to be conflict when the business does poorly. Failure often prompts a blame game, and the handshake turns into finger-pointing. Partners rarely see failure as a case of proportional mutual fault; thus recriminations ensue. So unless you are getting into business with the expectation of only so-so performance, you will need an agreement that covers what I call the vis-à-vis issues.

Your operating agreement with your partner should include all of the following provisions:

1. **Partner's roles and responsibilities.** The governance provision of your operating agreement should set forth each partner's role—for example, CEO or sales manager—and the partners' responsibilities within the business. The performance benchmarks and management responsibility for these roles should be covered in the partners' employment agreements. These provisions should also set forth how the partnership will make decisions. For example, you will need to determine which decisions will require a simple majority vote and which will require a unanimous vote. It's likely small capital expenditures and leasing low-cost assets can be decided by a majority vote,

whereas large capital expenditures and significant leasing or borrowing must be decided unanimously.

2. **Capital contributions.** The amount of capital to be contributed by each partner and under which circumstances future capital contributions will be required should be addressed. If one of the partners is going to be rewarded for "sweat equity," this too should be memorialized in the agreement. As we discussed previously, this type of equity is often in exchange for a "profits-only interest" to avoid immediate taxation.

3. **Ownership percentage, profit and loss percentages, and distributions.** The percentage ownership of capital and the relative percentages of profits and losses must be determined. As previously discussed, these must match when the entity is an S-Corporation, but they can be different with an LLC or partnership. Further, the cash distribution policy needs to be agreed upon. Generally partners determine the policy by agreeing on a percentage of total profits to be retained by the business and the amount and timing of the remaining cash to be distributed. At a minimum, distributions should cover the partners' tax liability on flow-through income from the partnership. Further, such payments should be made quarterly to match the due dates of estimated tax payments. There is no rule of thumb on the amounts retained versus distributed. It

is generally dependent on the facts and circumstances of the company, such as the partnership's capital expenditures budget and bank loan covenants.

4. **Partnership contingencies.** From the outset you must agree on what happens in the event a partner dies, becomes disabled, goes bankrupt, wants to leave, or wants to gift all or part of his or her interest. Let's take these in order. Generally, if a partner dies or becomes permanently disabled, the operating agreement requires the purchase of the deceased partner's interest. Since, in general, the remaining owner or owners would prefer not to be partners with a deceased or disabled partner's family members, the partnership or the partners individually agree to buy the interest at a value determined by an agreed-upon formula or an appraisal.

If a partner wishes to withdraw or becomes bankrupt, first the partnership and then the individual partners are given a right of first refusal, meaning the departing or bankrupt partner must first offer his or her interest to the partnership and then to the partners individually before being permitted to sell it to an outside, third party.

Gifting of interest is a particularly sticky issue because it often means the owners who are operating the business will be partnering with the natural objects of the departing partner's bounty and affection— generally a spouse, children, or a friend. This is a combustible mixture If this is to be permitted I strongly suggest the interest being placed in a voting trust with the trustee being approved by the majority of the remaining partners. This may sound like overkill, but believe me, it's not. If you've been paying attention, you now understand that operating a business even with a productive partner is no day at the beach; operating a business with your former partner's family or friends is at best a daunting task. As a result, limit your interactions to the voting trustee only. It's the best way to maintain your sanity and keep the business appropriately focused.

5. **Event of a sale.** You must agree upon what will happen if the company receives an offer from a buyer. Generally, selling the business requires unanimous consent, but if there are more than a couple of partners, the operating agreement can be drafted so a majority vote can approve the sale. It's not smart to give a minority partner veto power over an offer you shouldn't refuse. After all, every company will change hands eventually. So, even if your "liquidity event" doesn't coincide exactly with your scheduled retirement, you don't want a holdout sabotaging an otherwise good and profitable exit.

6. **Dissolution.** Lastly, you'll need to cover what happens if you and your partner just agree to disagree and the business must be dissolved. Dissolution generally requires the approval of a majority of the partners. Unanimity is not usually required, considering the dissolution is likely a result of the partners' inability to unanimously agree on anything. Upon dissolution all the property is either sold or distributed in liquidation of the partnership's business. In some instances, particularly if there is a partner who owns more than 50 percent of the business, he or she may be entitled to retain the business's name and use it in a subsequent venture.

Based upon the complexity of these issues, it is imperative to seek a topflight business attorney. Hiring a seasoned counselor is clearly the only way you will successfully "visualize" the many issues that may arise during the operation or cessation of your business. Please steer clear of online forms or hiring the lawyer on the corner who specializes in personal injury cases. Find an experienced attorney who has handled enough business matters to understand your business, as well as the partners' personalities and how they influence the operations—because they will. If you and your partner(s) spend considerable time thinking through these issues, come to a mutual understanding, and have an attorney add his or her wisdom to drafting a strong agreement, your chances for a long and mutually beneficial association increase exponentially.

NINE: Spigot Partners

Warning: The following is a word from your sponsor, a practicing CPA.

Forming partnerships with your professionals and bankers by keeping them well informed ensures you will be well advised. I know what you're thinking—advice from lawyers and CPAs is expensive. However, such advice, when sought judiciously, is valuable rather than expensive. Further, these partners and their costs are controlled by you. Think of them as a spigot that can be turned on and off as necessary. You control the information flow and therefore the cost. Since it is wholly your decision when the spigot of your professional partner needs to be turned on, it is important for you to recognize the critical times when you need to seek out the highly specialized advice of a seasoned lawyer or CPA. At these critical moments don't be afraid to turn on the spigot to receive value from your professionals, because this is when professional partners prove their worth by helping you avoid a big mistake.

Remember, you are in the race to win, so it's best to ride with a professional who has ridden the course many times before. So tuck in and draft behind your professional, increase your speed, and take absolutely the best route to the finish, because your professionals know the way.

The following are some attributes you should look for in your professional partners:

Fearless perspective. Because of their breadth of experience, professional partners don't scare easily. Unlike your internal team, who may be intimidated by you, these partners are paid to be analytical and detached. Furthermore, professionals run their own businesses every day in addition to helping others run theirs, so they have personally encountered many of your issues.

You should like them. Your professional partners should be people you like to spend time with as peers. Since you are going to be sharing dreams and aspirations with them over the course of many years, you might as well enjoy the necessary long conversations. Avoid professional partners who treat the partnership like a poor teacher-student relationship. If your professional partner doesn't call on you when your hand is raised, doesn't take the time to answer your questions, or genuinely doesn't know the answer, don't wait until the end of the semester to find a new partner. Finally, if the relationship is strictly professional and always "on the clock," the advice received will not have the nuance necessary for making just the right call.

Excellent listener. Implicit in the preceding attribute is finding a professional who's an excellent listener. I know based on my own dealings with lawyers that some like to bark out advice before they've heard the whole story. This is a bad sign because no two matters are exactly alike, and all require a full airing of the issues before a professional can render the correct advice.

Decisive. Next, avoid what a former law professor of mine called mugwumps. These advisers have their mugs on one side of the fence, their wumps on the other and as a result don't opine but only present options. Although presenting all options is important, having your partners tell you what they think you should do is critical and most valuable. Generally you can get the options from an internet posting or article. What you need is an opinion based on their considerable experience.

They can get to yes. Along these same lines, find professional partners who can tell you how something can be done rather than why you can't do it. The old maxim that you miss 100 percent of the shots you don't take is as true in business as it is in basketball, hockey, or soccer. If your professional partners consider themselves risk managers only, you risk missing out on opportunities. Moving a matter along to a "yes" is critical to growing a business. Advisers who either reason to a "no "or help you reason to a "no" are too afraid of being wrong. And those are not the kind of partners entrepreneurs need or want. Growing means getting to "yes"!

Understanding your advisers' why. Your professional partners' why is critical in your decision to partner with them or not. As thoroughly explained in Simon Sinek's book

Start with Why, the best partners, like the best companies, become the best because their customers and clients clearly understand why these professional partners are in business. Your professional partners' "why" is much more than just what they do and how they do it. Your partners' "why" should be to help you, in any way possible, achieve your business and personal financial goals. If they're in it only for their own business or financial goals, it will be obvious, as will be your need to look elsewhere.

OK, now that we have identified some attributes for your ideal professional partners, let's look at some examples of how specific professionals exhibit these attributes.

Lawyers: The best lawyers I know can see around corners and help you understand the potential unintended consequences of your actions. For example, you may believe your hotshot new sales guy will flee if you require him to sign a tight employment contract with an ironclad non-compete. A good lawyer will likely tell you what's standard and how far is too far in the employment agreement. The resulting agreement will be neither overly broad and unenforceable nor so onerous it has the unintended consequence of scaring your new sales guy away. The best attorneys provide the right level of protection for your rights, help you avoid litigation, and provide critical business insights. So don't scrimp.

CPAs: When you choose a CPA, find someone who will be an excellent financial coach. This means finding a CPA who truly cares about the success of your business and will take the time to understand it and your goals for it. The best accountants provide on-target advice, even when you may not want to hear it. They help you ensure your business meets or exceeds your industry's key performance indicators so you can maximize current profits and generate outstanding and durable value. As with lawyers, a CPA's ability to translate what she's learned from her largest clients to your business should supercharge your growth and profitability. When looking for a CPA, a great question to ask is, "Who is your biggest client and how did you help them grow?"

Bankers: Bankers may not be professional advice givers per se, but they are a significant source of valuable business intelligence. After all, it only makes sense to seek strategic input from a loan officer who has served larger and more successful companies than yours. Further, a consultative relationship with a banker allows you to understand what the bank will require your company to produce in terms of profits, growth, and equity in order to receive timely commitments and fair terms when borrowing money. And, let's face it, no matter how great your company's success, access to capital on advantageous terms will always be necessary to fuel growth.

I cannot guarantee that hiring the correct professional partners will propel your business to unprecedented success. However, I can guarantee they will prevent you from making a big mistake, which at least gives you the *chance* for unprecedented success. While professional partners will never know your business like you do, the best ones will get darn close. When you partner with professionals who graft what you know about your business and industry to their likely fifty-thousand-plus hours of handling business issues, you have created a superstrong doubles team—one that should win most matches easily.

CONCLUSION: Your Company, Your Call!

So there is an "us" in business after all. But if you take away nothing else from this book, please give every alternative to partnering higher priority. This is particularly true if you, like most entrepreneurs, decided to buy or start a business because of your strong belief in the correctness of your ideas and your even stronger need to implement them yourself. Slowing down to check with or convince a partner just might act as a governor on your business that would otherwise be turbocharged. Even though going it alone may make those early years of business ownership feel like dog years, in my considerable experience, most entrepreneurs who decided to go it alone were happier later.

Business is a financial undertaking with obvious emotional results, not an emotional undertaking with financial results. Keep this straight.

Remember, partnering should be reserved for the acquisition of a rare skill rather than a knee-jerk reaction to fear of the unknown or the need for capital. Exhaust all non-partner avenues for skills and capital rather than settling for what feels most comfortable.

To be a successful entrepreneur, you need to be able to live with uncertainty, because there is no finish line labeled SUCCESS. So you might as well get used to living with uncertainty from the get-go. It may seem trite, but the old adage that success is a journey and not a destination is true. That journey will have fewer detours and be far more fun and certainly more financially rewarding if you're at the wheel without a backseat driver or a flat tire partner.

It's your life, your business, and your decision. Remember, adding a partner later, when you know you need one, is far easier and cheaper than expelling one you didn't need.

PATRICK J. BURKE

Patrick Burke, a CPA and attorney, is the managing partner of Burke & Schindler, CPAs, a firm he founded in 1984. Since the firm's inception, Burke has continuously recruited the most talented professionals to broaden the scope of the practice and to ensure Burke & Schindler clients receive top-notch service. The firm specializes in business consulting, taxation, audit and accounting, executive recruiting and staffing, and retirement plan administration.

Burke is a respected expert in business acquisitions and sales, deal structuring, value building and succession planning. In addition, he has advised more than 200 highly successful start-ups. His commitment to a proactive approach has earned him the trust and respect of his clients. He exceeds expectations by becoming clients' go-to business adviser.

Burke has been a featured lecturer on entrepreneurship at The University of Dayton and numerous seminars. He is a former member of the "Forty Under 40" business leaders in Cincinnati and a member of the Ohio Society of Certified Public Accountants, the American Institute of Certified

Public Accountants, the Ohio and American Bar Associations.

Currently, he is Chairman of the board of directors of a closely held $70 million medical consulting company and board member (including chairman of the audit and compensation committees) of a closely held $500 million real estate services business and holds Series 7 and Series 63 licenses.

Burke received his J.D. from the University of Cincinnati Law School and his B.S. cum laude from the University of Dayton.

Outside of work, Patrick is active with Boys Hope Girls Hope of Cincinnati, Catholic Inner City Schools Education Fund (CISE) and The Dynamic Catholic Institute.

If you'd like help buying a business,
running the one you have more profitably,
or selling your business for top dollar,
please contact Patrick Burke:

www.burkecpa.com
901 Adams Crossing
Cincinnati, OH 45202
513-455-8200
business@burkecpa.com